Sharing Wisdom
Across the Ages

Sharing Wisdom Across the Ages

FROM ELEMENTARY SCHOOL TO RETIREMENT

Steve Piscitelli

The Growth and Resilience Network®

Also written by Steve Piscitelli

Roxie Looks for Purpose Beyond the Biscuit
Community as a Safe Place to Land
Stories about Teaching, Learning, and Resilience:
No Need to be an Island
Choices for College Success (1ˢᵗ, 2ⁿᵈ, and 3ʳᵈ editions)
Study Skills: Do I Really Need This Stuff?
(1ˢᵗ, 2ⁿᵈ, and 3ʳᵈ editions)
Engaging Activities for Student Success
I Don't Need This Stuff! Or Do I?
A Study Skills and Time Management Book
Does Anyone Understand This Stuff?
A Student Guide to Organizing United States History.
(1ˢᵗ and 2ⁿᵈ editions)

Dedication

To Roxie.
Thank you for your guidance, patience,
companionship, and quiet wisdom.

Contents

Gratitude

I APPRECIATE EVERY PERSON WHO took the time to reflect on the questions, compose their answers, and send them to me. Without their input, there would be no book. There also have been those who graciously shared their time by reviewing and critiquing the manuscript drafts. If anyone asked that their contributions remain anonymous, I honored that request. I have not included professional titles, academic degrees, gender identification, or marital status with the names—just first and last names (and when provided a middle initial or name).

I am grateful to the following (in alphabetical order by the first name):

Alexander "Sandy" Berry, Anjali Jain Lueck, Ann Pearson, Ashli Archer, B. Starr Simpson, Bob Fuller, Brian Crawford, Brian Heggood, Bruce Cleary, Cass Tillis Worthington, Chris Hopper, Chris Lester, Christopher Bartlett, Clare Aronow,

Curtis Ford, Dan Whitford, Dane Gilbert, Dave Black, David R. Johnson, David Tracy, Don R. Lynn, Eileen Krimsky, Ellen Glasser, Evan Kraus, Fran Bartlett, Frances Bartlett Kinne, Frances Mascola, Gary Bilderback, Hillary Perry Coley, Irene Kovala, Jackie Fuller, Jacquie Ott, Janet Kemmerer, Janet Quigley-Abbott, Jennifer Billman, Joan S. Carver, Jo Gilbert, Joe Cuseo, John J. "SKI" Sygielski, Joseph Robinson, Jr., Kamilla Wieckowski, Kathy Hodges, Kim Rinaman, L. Marshall Washington, Lana G. Rinaman, Laurie Piscitelli, Leonard Lay, Linnie S. Carter, Lisa Duke, Lori Sundberg, Lynne Norton, Maria Mark, Mark Johnson, Matthew Mitchell, Mike Hall, Mike Molla, Mordecai Ian Brownlee, Neftali Perez, Paul Herman, Preston Hodges, Robin Fitzpatrick, Rodneiyka Thornton, Roz Hoffman, St. Joseph's Catholic School 2nd grade class of Cass Tillis Worthington, Sally Clemens, Scott Esser, Sharon Scholl, Stanton College Preparatory School selected sophomore and senior students of Brian Heggood, Steve Nunez, Thomas Long, Timothy Sandoe, Todd Hoover, Toni Cleveland, and Veronica Thomas-Gladden.

Tying Your Shoes
and Wisdom

WHAT DOES WISDOM MEAN?

The answer to that question differs from person to person, group to group, and day to day. We can define wisdom as insight, good judgment, common sense, and wise action. I think, however, you can see the rub. What you consider insight, good judgment, common sense, and wise action will be viewed by someone else as lacking in all those qualities.

When I asked a second-grade class what advice[1] younger students need to consider, six words came from one of the students.

Learn How to Tie Your Shoes!

---

[1] This book presents answers to three questions concerning wisdom. "Advice" was the subject of one of the questions. For more information, read pages 13-14, "The Wisdom-Seeking Questions."

On the surface, the answer seems cute, obvious, and lacking wisdom. "Of course, we need to learn to tie our shoes!" you might say. Someone else might counter with, "No need to do that. I wear slip-on loafers!"

I'd suggest we pause, move beyond the literal words, and consider a deeper meaning. Does the statement conjure images of personal growth or individual freedom? After all, when we learned to tie our shoes, we became more independent from our parents. We walked with less fear of tripping on the laces by securing those loops and knots.

The point? No matter how old or young the wisdom sharer may be, his or her words can hold a deeper meaning. Are we ready to allow those thoughts to enter our minds for consideration?

As you read the more-than 300 responses on the following pages, can you see similar and different perspectives between and within age groups? Who determines which of those is wise and what is not? What is the rubric? Is wisdom contingent upon where we stand and what our experiences have been? Or is wisdom fluid and ever-changing?

We can all benefit when we acknowledge and embrace that the light of wisdom shines from generation to generation.

The Inspiration

⤜⤛⤛⤚

INITIALLY, I ENVISIONED THIS BOOK as a compilation of octo-genarian (people in their 80s) wisdom. The initial inspiration came a few days after Christmas 2020. A block from the ocean. A few minutes after sunrise.

Most mornings, my canine partner, Roxie, and I find ourselves on the beach, toes (and paws) in the sand, watching the sun rise above the ocean. Promise and opportunity for another day of life. A safe place to gather my thoughts and take a deep breath of appreciation.

Returning home that morning in 2020, we ran into Baby and her person, Bob. Baby, a mixed breed with a greying snout, is one of Roxie's canine buds. After they greeted each other with sniffs and wiggles, both dogs sat in front of me, looking for the expected biscuit. Bob, a retired US Navy submariner, scratched Roxie's haunches. On this day, Bob had a gift for my wife and me. A home-made rum cake from his wife, Jackie.

"I tried to deliver this to your house but ended up at the wrong address," he said as he handed me the gift-wrapped offering. "The lady was nice, but she wasn't about to get your cake!"

We shared a few laughs; I thanked Bob and returned home, my mouth watering for the treat that was to complement my morning coffee.

As I nibbled (ok, gobbled) the first slice, my thoughts returned to Bob and Jackie. Both are active, in-shape, and sharp-minded octogenarians. Bob graduated from the Naval Academy as a classmate of John McCain. He always seems to have something going on around the house. And he and Baby walk each day. Jackie is active in her church. Both always have pleasant greetings and broad smiles for us when we meet. On that morning—the rum cake day—I wondered what advice they and other octogenarians might have for the younger generations. After nearly nine full decades of life experiences, what are their takeaways from life's journey? What lessons have they learned? Have the lessons changed over the years, or have they become etched in stone?

And what questions do they have as they look toward entry into the nonagenarian (people in their 90s) club?

I did some reading about the oldest of the old and started drafting ideas about a book of advice and questions from the perspective of the eighty-year-olds in our country. What could we learn from eighty-plus years of living? What could I learn?

Hoping to tap into the wisdom of the ages, I developed an initial list of more than sixty questions. Like:

* What has been the most important lesson you have learned and would like to pass along to people younger than you?
* What has been the most significant societal change you have experienced?
* As you have aged, how have you moved from merely surviving to striving and thriving?
* What is the best way to navigate life's journey?
* If your thirty-year-old self sat down with you for a conversation today, what do you think would surprise him or her the most about the eighty-year-old sitting in front of him or her?
* If you could only share one piece of advice or wisdom, what would it be?
* How do you stay socially connected?
* As you look ahead to your nineties what questions do you have?

And so on.

At the same time I was developing these questions, I heard Amanda Gorman, a twenty-two-year-old with recollections, lessons, and questions, deliver her poignant 2021 presidential inaugural poetry reading. The obvious occurred to me:

We can receive wisdom from all age groupings.

Their perspectives may be different. *Vicenarians* (people in their 20s) and *Quinquagenarians* (people in their 50s) may experience a career change but do their views differ about that occupational shift? And if they do differ, in what ways? Do three decades of separation create a different worldview? How about six or seven decades? Can we find lessons in that separation that speak to us as common humanity?

And what about the *Denarians* (10- to 19-year-olds)? They have learned lessons, and they have questions. Don't they have something to share in this conversation?

I believe they do.

And so, this book developed. More than a book of decades, this is a book of people in those decades. A book of their recollections, lessons, and questions.

A ROUND OF GOLF

One of the memorable lines from the film *Forrest Gump* has the lead character sharing wisdom with a woman sitting beside him at a Savannah bus stop.

> *"Life is like a box of chocolates. You never know what you're going to get."*

Here's another wisdom simile I offer for your consideration:

> *Life is like a round of golf. Each hole brings a new view.*

The golfer starts at the 1st tee, and she makes her way around the course encountering open fairways, sand traps, water hazards, trees, and, depending on the location, perhaps an alligator or two. Each hole, obstacle, swing, success, and challenge provides experience for the next hole. While all eighteen holes occupy the same course, the experiences gained from each stroke, fairway, and putting green bring different perspectives. Finally, as the golfer walks the fairway toward the green on the last hole, she has an entire round to reflect upon. When the ball drops in the cup, the match is over. The "19th hole" awaits.

As of 2019 (according to CDC statistics), United States life expectancy came in just shy of 79 years[2]. Staying with our golfing simile means each hole equates to about 4.4 years. The golfer turning from the 9th green to the 10th tee has lived (using these metrics) for almost forty years.

---

2 "National Vital Statistics System: NCHS Fact Sheet," National Center for Health Statistics, March 2021. https://www.cdc.gov/nchs/data/factsheets/factsheet_nvss.pdf. Accessed September 17, 2022. And "U.S. Life Expectancy 1950-2022," Macrotrends, n.d. https://www.macrotrends.net/countries/USA/united-states/life-expectancy. Accessed September 17, 2022. Also, considering the impact of COVID, overall US life expectancy dropped to 76.1 years on average according to "Vital Statistics Rapid Release," U.S. Department of Health and Human Services, Centers for Disease Control and Prevention, National Center for Health Statistics, National Vital Statistics System, Report No. 23, August 2022. https://www.cdc.gov/nchs/data/vsrr/vsrr023.pdf. Accessed September 17, 2022.

She is at midlife, looking back and reflecting as she tees up for the back nine.

At this writing, I am sixty-nine years old. I've "played" about sixteen holes with two left before I exit (staying with the CDC metrics). My view will likely differ from someone on other tees, fairways, and greens who had different experiences and a better or inferior set of clubs.

Regardless of where we stand or where we venture, we have recollections, lessons, and questions. We need to respect each group and the wisdom it has to offer our respective communities. Or, at the least, engage in conversations to better understand differing perspectives.

THE DECADES

I gathered (non-scientific) information through personal interviews, emails, phone calls, survey forms, and letters from the following age groupings[3].

- *Kiddiegenarians*[4] (9-year-olds & under)
- *Denarians* (10- to 19-year-olds)
- *Vicenarians* (20- to 29-year-olds)

---

3 See Charles Patrick Davis (ed), "Medical Definition of Age by Decade." MedicineNet, March 21, 2021. https://www.medicinenet.com/age_by_decade/definition.htm. Accessed September 17, 2022. Also, see Charles Patrick Davis, "Definition of Age by Decade." The Rx List, March 29, 2021. https://www.rxlist.com/age_by_decade/definition.htm. Accessed September 17, 2022.

4 This label was improvised by the author.

- *Tricenarians* (30- to 39-year-olds)
- *Quadragenarians* (40- to 49-year-olds)
- *Quinquagenarians* (50- to 59-year-olds)
- *Sexagenarians* (60- to 69-year-olds)
- *Septuagenarians* (70- to 79-year-olds)
- *Octogenarians* (80- to 89-year-olds)
- *Nonagenarians* (90- to 99-year-olds)
- *Centenarians* (100- to 109-year-olds)

No matter where *you* fall in these decades, you can learn from each group. And *we* can learn from you.

METHODOLOGY AND LIMITATIONS OF THIS "STUDY"

The following pages do *not* present a scientific study. What you will read does *not* represent probability, random, systemic, stratified, or cluster sampling. Other than my attempt to get responses from people in each age group noted above, my sampling and reporting would not stand up to an analytic test. To be sure, I identified eleven populations (the age groups) and then sought out respondents (the samples) from each population. One-hundred-twenty-seven people submitted responses to the three questions. You will read more than three hundred offerings of wisdom in the following pages.

I (a sexagenarian) reached out to groups in my various communities. I sought people from retirement centers, governing councils, spiritual congregations, hospice centers, volunteer groups, the business community, the television industry, higher education, neighbors, elementary and high school students, former colleagues, colleagues of colleagues, neighbors, friends, and friends of friends.

This "sampling method" did lead to a few challenges. Just under 40% of the respondents fall into the 50-year-old to 90-year-old groupings. 51% were elementary and senior high students. Despite my outreach to younger contacts, I gathered just a few responses (about 9%) from the 20- to 49-year-old groupings. Perhaps the wisdom lesson here is how our social and professional contacts tend to decrease in diversity as we retire and age. And so do our opportunities to engage with different perspectives and world views.

To read more about the demographic makeup of these respondents, see Appendix A: The Demographics.

THE WHY? A DEEPER DIVE

So, why write this book, given the sampling shortcomings noted above? For one, we learn more lessons as we gather and contemplate insights from various demographics. And, hopefully, we become more curious about and appreciative of our neighbors. Conversations and deliberative dialogues can develop.

The hope is that this book stimulates conversations amongst and between the age groups. We live in (have created for ourselves?) a time where common ground looks to be ever more elusive. The go-to point often seems to dismiss differing viewpoints, failing to see that each brings a different perspective and unique wisdom to the conversation.

This book provides a glimpse into those different perspectives. Rather than dismiss, let's attempt to understand.

The Conversation

At the end of each age grouping in this book, you will find a question to consider:

> *What conclusions can you draw about this*
> *group's lessons, advice, or questions?*

Before you move on to the next age group and set of responses, take a few moments to contemplate that question and record your answers.

At the end of each section of the book (after reading all of the age groups' responses to the question at hand), you will find three questions to consider:

* *What similarities did you detect from group to group?*
* *What differences stood out between the age groups?*

* *What takeaway(s) do you have after reading the wisdom responses?*

Please take the time to talk with friends, colleagues, and community members about what you have read in this book. Perhaps it will encourage you to do a similar project in your community, workplace, or family.

The Wisdom-
Seeking Questions

THE PARTICIPANTS FOR THIS BOOK all responded to the same three questions.[5] The wording might have been a little different depending on the age group. For instance, rather than asking eight-year-olds to wax philosophic about what they had learned thus far in their lives, I found that asking them to describe their most important second-grade lesson had more resonance. In general,

5 All respondents submitted their wisdom responses to the author by email, via US postal service, via face-to-face interview, or by verbally sharing their responses. All respondents gave me their permission to publish their words, names, and age group-ing. A review of submitted responses has been done by the author and various proofreaders. In a few instances, some wording was changed for brevity or stylistic reasons. Effort was made to keep the intent of the provided wisdom unchanged. If any error or omission has occurred, it is inadvertent, and corrections will be made (provided that written notification is made to the author) in any future editions of this book. All respondents were asked to submit their words, not those of others.

each person who responded to this book answered a variation of:

1. What do you see as the biggest **LESSON** you have learned to this point of your life?
2. What one piece of **ADVICE** would you like to pass along to the younger people following in your footsteps?
3. As you look ahead to your future, what one **QUESTION** would you like to ask those who are older than you?

You will find answers from the respondents for each question. I asked them to use their words. I did not want them to offer a quote from another source to answer any of the questions. I have accepted their promise that what they have submitted (their wording) is their original contribution.

One reviewer of this book's manuscript observed that the Kiddiegenarians probably repeated words learned from adults. Might we draw a similar conclusion for other groups? Is it possible that all of us have internalized important lessons, readings, or teachings we now repeat as our wisdom?

Read the words. Compare the age groups. What differences jump out? What similarities do you notice? What conclusions can you draw? What conversations can you start? What can we learn?

The Demographic Groups[6]

❧

Kiddiegenarians[7]
(9-year-olds & under)
Percentage of Total Population in the USA:
Approximately 11.8%

❧

---

6 "American Community Survey S0101: Age and Sex," United States Census Bureau, 2021. https://data.census.gov/cedsci/table?q=population%20by%20age%20groups&tid=ACSST1Y2021.S0101. Accessed September 18, 2022. Also, see "Our Changing Population: United States," USA Facts, July 2022. US population by year, race, age, ethnicity, & more | USAFacts. Accessed September 18, 2022. The author has rounded numbers. Both sources placed the 2021 population just under 332,000,000. The percentages are offered here as one way to view the population distribution in the USA by age. NOTE: Both sources did not separate numbers for the octogenarian, nonagenarian, and centenarian populations.

7 See footnote #4.

Denarians
(10- to 19-year-olds)
Percentage of Total Population in the USA:
Approximately 12.9%

Vicenarians
(20– to 29-year-olds)
Percentage of Total Population in the USA:
Approximately 13.8%

Tricenarians
(30– to 39-year-olds)
Percentage of Total Population in the USA:
Approximately 13.7%

Quadragenarians
(40- to 49-year-olds)
Percentage of Total Population in the USA:
Approximately 12.3%

Quinquagenarians
(50- to 59-year-olds)
Percentage of Total Population in the USA: Approximately 13.2%

Sexagenarians
(60- to 69-year-olds)
Percentage of Total Population in the USA: Approximately 11.9%

Septuagenarians
(70- to 79-year-olds)
Percentage of Total Population in the USA: Approximately 7.6%

Octogenarians, Nonagenarians, and Centenarians
(80- to 109-year-olds)
Percentage of Total Population in the USA: Approximately 3.7%

Takeaways and Lessons: A Challenge to the Reader

❧

EACH TIME I READ AND re-read the words in the following pages, I came away with new insights. Same words but a shift in perspective. As I reviewed the responses, a few themes appeared within each group. I have provided my takeaways at the end of this book.

Please do not read those yet. Draw your conclusions. Discuss with colleagues, family, community members, a book club, and friends. Listen to what they gleaned from the shared wisdom.

When it comes to the wisdom of the ages, did anything stand out to you? What surprised you? What confirmed previously held beliefs? Has your perspective shifted, or an opinion changed? What lessons did you learn? What advice would you now give? What question moves to the front of your mind?

Finally, what would you include if you were to write a follow-up book (your book about wisdom)?

I would love to hear your thoughts.

The Lessons

❦

What do you see as the biggest LESSON you have learned to this point of your life?

Kiddiegenarians[8]

❧

Encourage others when they feel they can't do it.
(2nd Grader)

We received instructions on the proper way to receive
First Holy Communion.
(2nd Grader)

Treat others the way you want to be treated.
(2nd Grader)

Learn from your mistakes.
(2nd Grader)

Become the best version of yourself.
(2nd Grader)

---

8 All of the responses of the first two groups, Kiddiegenarians
and Denarians, (all less than 18 years of age) were submitted
without names. They came to the author anonymously.

Keep on trying.
(2nd Grader)

Get closer to God.
(2nd Grader)

Pray daily.
(2nd Grader)

When someone says they're sorry, forgive them!
(2nd Grader)

Never give up.
(2nd Grader)

Our teacher loves us.
(2nd Grader)

Our teacher is the best version of herself.
(2nd Grader)

❧

What conclusions can you draw
about this group's lessons?

Denarians[9]

❦

Do and go what/where makes you happy. If you need a
different environment to thrive and survive, do everything you need to get there and work hard.
(High school senior)

Hard work pays off.
(High school senior)

Care enough to succeed, but not too much
to be disappointed enough to spiral.
(High school senior)

The importance of discipline and perseverance.
(High school senior)

Be patient with others but know when and
how to set boundaries. Essentially, know how to

_____

9 Refer to footnote number 8.

communicate your thoughts,
feelings, and intentions.
(High school senior)

Work hard and make sure you have the discipline
to keep working hard.
(High school senior)

Stop caring about those overarching goals you happen
to come into rather than those you want to achieve.
(High school senior)

Showing up is half the battle.[10]
(High school senior)

Do what you want when you want. You are the only person in charge of your direction.
(High school senior)

Perfectionism is stupid. The best work you make
comes after endless mistakes.
(High school senior)

Living in any way where another's opinion dictates your
own is the quickest way to frustration.
Also, eating peanut butter is good.
(High school senior)

---

10 Also attributed to Stephen Hawking.

If you don't think you can do something, remember
there is some absolute moron that is doing it just fine
and getting away with it.
(High school senior)

Work towards what you want, think positively,
and truly believe it will happen.
(High school senior)

Stress is important, but too much stress
starts a cycle of stress.
(High school senior)

Don't hold back from trying new things out of fear of
failure.
(High school senior)

Nothing in life comes easily.[11]
(High school senior)

Turn nothing into something.
(High school senior)

I learned how to stay focused on my passions.
(High school senior)

---

11 Teddy Roosevelt is reported to have said something similar:
"Nothing worth having comes easy."

The village eats before you do.[12]
(High school senior)

Everything we are is insignificant,
but that makes our lives worth living.[13]
(High school senior)

How to manage time.
(High school senior)

Hard work doesn't always pay off. There are always
things outside of my control.
(High school senior)

Never fail to try more.
Not everything that calls your name is for you.
(High school sophomore)

The best thing to learn from high school other than
academics is friendship. Knowing who your friends truly
are can benefit your mental health.
(High school sophomore)

---

12 You may have seen variations of this in leadership literature. One source is Simon Sinek, *Leaders Eat Last: Why Some Teams Pull Together and Others Don't.* New York: Penguin Group, 2014.

13 Mahatma Gandhi also receives credit for similar thoughts about the significance and insignificance of life.

If you do it last minute, it only takes a minute to do.[14]
(High school sophomore)

Kindness can do wonders, no matter how big or small.
(High school sophomore)

My biggest lesson is never to diminish my trauma
because someone has had it worse.
(High school sophomore)

You can't wait around and expect things to change.
(High school sophomore)

Say yes to more. Saying no only hinders your capability
to make new experiences that you can learn from.
(High school sophomore)

I have learned that some days just don't go as planned.
The most important ability is the one to adapt.
(High school sophomore)

One lesson I have learned to this point in life
is never to judge people.
(High school sophomore)

---

14 In addition to a few book titles, you might have seen a version
of this referred to as "Parkinson's Law."

To improve, you must make mistakes.
(High school sophomore)

I feel the biggest lesson I've learned in my life
is to live in the moment.
(High school sophomore)

Appreciate what you have. That includes people, opportunities, and situations that might seem difficult to go
through.
(High school sophomore)

Surround yourself with five smart people
and you will be the sixth.[15]
(High school sophomore)

*What conclusions can you draw
about this group's lessons?*

---

15 You may have seen this with "intelligent" or "confident" in place of "smart."

Vicenarians

⬿

I used to be in such a rush and hurry to grow up, losing some great moments and experiences along the way. When I lost my grandmother, who raised me, I realized the importance of enjoying life's moments because you don't want to look back one day with regrets wishing you had more time.
(Rodneiyka Thornton)

Be yourself. Life is too short to be concerned with the opinions of others. You can't please everyone.
(Chris Hopper)

Do not compare yourself to other people. Set goals for yourself and focus on achieving them.
(Evan Kraus)

Adults aren't perfect and make mistakes.
(Kamilla Wieckowski)

*What conclusions can you draw
about this group's lessons?*

Tricenarians

Believe what people show you.
Actions truly speak louder than words.
(Mordecai Ian Brownlee)

Not everyone shares the same morals.
(Neftali Perez)

What conclusions can you draw
about this group's lessons?

Quadragenarians

Wise people feel, listen, read, consider, apply, reconsider, and pivot with new data and context.
(Anjali Jain Lueck)

The more I've learned, the less I realize I know. The world and most of its issues are complex and require deep, patient, compassionate, and open-minded deliberation.
(Todd Hoover)

Be flexible during this life journey. Change is constant, not just in the environment and technological advances but also in individuals. We are not the same people we were at ages 18, 21, and 30. We are growing and adapting as people through each stage of life and the lessons we learned at that time.
(Veronica Thomas-Gladden)

Question everything and everyone, including yourself.
Asking "Why?" is the most powerful thing you can do
before acting or speaking.
(Hillary Perry Coley)

You can't abdicate your responsibility to think for yourself to someone else. Most people rely on what they've
been told without properly
investigating matters themselves.
(Leonard Lay)

Say "Yes" a lot. Not to tasks or obligations
but opportunities.
You never know what doors may open.
(Clare Aronow)

❦

What conclusions can you draw
about this group's lessons?

Quinquagenarians

You can never tell what someone else is dealing with
at any particular moment. Hedge your bets and just
be kind all the time, so you don't make a bad day even
worse with a hurtful comment.
(Ann Pearson)

Don't take it personally. Some people are angry, trou-
bled, or depressed. It has very little to do with you.
(Matthew Mitchell)

There is no such thing as destiny or fate. So, make
choices and live with the consequences of your choices,
especially when it comes to being open or vulnerable to
love. Most people get at least one chance at true love in
their lives. If they grab it and hold on to it, it will, in the
end, conquer all—even hate and evil.
(Mark Johnson)

Personal success is not a one-person job. The people with whom we choose to be close can provide support and challenges. Find your people and spend time with those who want to see you succeed. One must make good choices and put the work in every single day. There is no quick path to success.
The path is what is important.
(Robin Fitzpatrick)

Put your "oxygen mask" on first. You cannot help others if you cannot help yourself first.
(Linnie S. Carter)

My dad always said to "never move away from a job, but always move towards a job."
So don't get frustrated or angry or whatever, then up and quit, until you have secured a new opportunity.
(Mike Hall)

We don't live our lives with nearly enough "grace" for our self-expectations and, more importantly, others.
(Mike Molla)

Life is a journey with ups and downs like a roller coaster. Enjoy the ride because you only go around once...Follow passion and work with incredible people.
That will lead to happiness.
(Scott Esser)

Treat people with kindness and respect, and recognize
that you never know what weight others carry.
Not everything is about you.
(Steve Nunez)

Just because the answer is clear does not mean
you deny people an opportunity to weigh into
the final answer.
(L. Marshall Washington)

Contentment doesn't stem from control over self,
others, or circumstances. Contentment stems from a
commitment to demonstrable acts of compassion,
forgiveness, grace, and generosity.
(Jennifer Billman)

Our life's journey is unpredictable...Societal and political forces can change work and life environments more
quickly than ever before, and we need
to adapt to the changing landscapes.
(David Tracy)

I am not what others say I am.
I am responsible for my own identity.
(B. Starr Simpson)

We are created with a purpose. You will have a good life
if you can find your purpose, passion, and people.
(Dan Whitford)

✺

*What conclusions can you draw
about this group's lessons?*

Sexagenarians

Believe in myself.
(John J. "Ski" Sygielski)

All my past experiences and decisions
have prepared me to be right here, right now.
(Maria Mark)

Many people experience a metaphoric shipwreck. Their
boat busts apart, yet they manage to float onward on
a remnant. It may be that you require less than you
thought you did
to reach your destiny.
(Paul Herman)

Life can and will change in a heartbeat.
(Bruce Cleary)

Although it may not be obvious,
everyone has their backstory.
No one is immune to struggles and challenges.
(Janet Kemmerer)

Get your education. No one can take that
away from you.
(Chris Lester)

Don't take yourself too seriously.
(Curtis Ford)

Life and our ecosystem on Earth are fragile. Make
choices like your future depends on those decisions.
(Timothy Sandoe)

It is important to treat others with respect
if you want it in return.
You have an opportunity every day
to impact others with kindness.
(Thomas Long)

Life is short and what may have been important in my
younger years is not as important today. I try not to
get overwhelmed by or overreact to difficult issues or
concerns.
After all, most problems are short-term and only
temporary.
(Anonymous)

Listen more, talk less…Speak your mind but do it politely… Everyone has their perspective on all things in life….
(Dave Black)

Age is just a number.
(Janet Quigley-Abbott)

To keep my own counsel.
What others think of me is none of my business.
I need to do what I believe is right and is my calling.
(Lori Sundberg)

The time to make a friend is before you need one.
(Joseph Robinson, Jr.)

Don't wait until you are ready to take a big step because you might never be ready…Seek support and find mentors to help you act. Reward requires risk. You will make mistakes, but it is worth it.
(Ellen Glasser)

❧

What conclusions can you draw about this group's lessons?

Septuagenarians

❦

COVID taught me how incredibly lucky I am/we are. We have each other, friends, family, homes, food, health, an amazing beach, and books.
(Eileen Krimsky)

It is important to seek and maintain balance in my life. Be more careful about attending to all key components of my "self"—physical, social, emotional, and vocational.
(Joe Cuseo)

Life is what you and your Lord make it!
(Lana G. Rinaman)

Let those who are most affected by a decision make the decision.
(Lynne Norton)

Those difficult times you think will sink you bear gifts
if you are patient and open to receiving them. For
example, the heartbreaking experience of losing a
three-month-old son has allowed me, as a counselor and
a friend, to simply sit with people who have experienced
loss without needing to fix them, trusting that they will
heal.
(Kathy Hodges)

Faith in God gives meaning and purpose to life.
And service to humanity is the greatest work of life.
(Don R. Lynn)

Empathic listening is the key to successful relationships.
When I live that lesson, all is well, but when I don't,
the opportunity for a relationship dies.
(Preston Hodges)

Never burn bridges. The person who slighted you today
may be the one who will save you in the future.
(Toni Cleveland)

The little things in life are the big things. An unexpected call from a friend. A book you read before becomes a new friend. An old photo from the past... Standing on the shore and feeling small.

(Irene Kovala)

◦⊷∞⊶◦

*What conclusions can you draw
about this group's lessons?*

Octogenarians

Life will unfold according to natural law
and human action.
No vast benevolent power will come to the rescue.
(Sharon Scholl)

Be open, listen, pray, and act.
(Sally Clemens)

Love God, myself, and others.
(Kim Rinaman)

I cannot solve all problems confronting me, so I seek
alternatives from others.
(David R. Johnson)

The physical universe is continuously changing, as do the cultural, political, and intellectual environments. And one's physical condition changes daily. Happiness and contentment in life are more certain if impermanence is understood and accepted. The wise figure this out; those that don't, and more significantly, those that deny impermanence, constantly suffer.
(Alexander "Sandy" Berry)

You can be proud of who you are and what you accomplish but also be humble. Humility can rein in tendencies to excessive pride. Periods of arrogance in my life have invariably led to grief. (Bob Fuller)[16]

❦

What conclusions can you draw about this group's lessons?

---

16 This is Bob from the beginning of this book. See the section, "The Inspiration."

Nonagenarians

⚜

I am struck by how short life is and how quickly the
years go by. When one is young, the end of life seems far
away. Then suddenly, it is close by. Time is our most pre-
cious commodity, so we should use it well. Don't waste
time regretting the past. Find a balance that works for
you between work and home.
(Joan S. Carver)

My parents always taught me to be independent. And
I had a general optimism about my capacity to live
unhampered
by doubt, hesitation, or fear.
(Frances Bartlett Kinne)[17]

---

17 Two points here. (1) Frances Bartlett Kinne and Fran Bartlett
are two separate individuals. They are not related. (2) At the time
of this publication, Frances Bartlett Kinne had passed away at
the age of 102. She shared her comments with the author during a podcast they recorded when she was 99 years old. See Steve
Piscitelli, "Episode #20: Life is not About Me, It's About Others.

Let your kids develop their wisdom. Don't project yours
on them. They need to learn to fly from the nest.
(Fran Bartlett)

Be close to family. Give all you can.
(Frances Mascola)

❧

*What conclusions can you draw
about this group's lessons?*

(100 Years of Insight)," The Growth and Resilience Network®,
November 15, 2016. https://youtu.be/-XK6ZOuO-os. Accessed
on September 26, 2022.

Centenarians

❦

Find something you like
that keeps you physically active.[18]
(Jo Gilbert)

❦

*What conclusions can you draw
about this centenarian lesson?*

---

18 Since Jo Gilbert is the eldest respondent for this book, here is an interesting note about her journey as presented to the author by her son, Dane Gilbert: "She was on the USA Lawn Bowling team competing all over the world. She is in the Lawn Bowling Hall of Fame. Both of my parents lawn bowled well into their 80s."

Takeaways and Perspectives

❦

BEFORE YOU MOVE ON TO the next section, pause and reflect on the responses you just read. Engage a friend, colleague, family member, or community representative in a dialogue for their perspectives. Use the following as conversation starters:

- What similarities did you detect from group to group?
- What striking differences stood out between the age groups?
- What takeaway(s) do you have after reading the wisdom responses?

The Advice

❦

What one piece of ADVICE would you like to pass along to the younger generations—those who represent the future?

Kiddiegenarians

Learn how to tie your shoes!
(2nd Grader)

Know how to "regroup" in math.
(2nd Grader)

Know math.
(2nd Grader)

Know what you are going to do in
First Holy Communion.
(2nd Grader)

Learn phonics and doubles facts.
(2nd Grader)

Spell properly.
(2nd Grader)

Know how to read.
(2nd Grader)

Write pretty and neat.
(2nd Grader)

Learn how to subtract.
(2nd Grader)

Have manners and be polite.
(2nd Grader)

Take textbooks out of your desk neatly.
(2nd Grader)

Be the best version of yourself.
(2nd Grader)

Don't talk when the teacher is talking.
(2nd Grader)

Don't do dangerous things.
(2nd Grader)

On the first day of school, don't be afraid. Don't think
it's going to be harder than it is.
(2nd Grader)

Watch how you number your test pages.
(2nd Grader)

Remember to say "Hi" when you walk into the room.
(2nd Grader)

Use capitals and periods.
(2nd Grader)

*What conclusions can you draw
about this group's advice?*

Denarians

❦

It's your future on the line, so don't mess it up trying to
look cool or please someone else.
(High school senior)

Just push through, no matter how unmotivated you feel.
(High school senior)

Find good friends and be a good friend.
(High school senior)

Everything happens for a reason.
So, don't dwell on things you can't control.
(High school senior)

Be resilient. Look after yourself. You are responsible
for your own emotions and words. Make sure you take
responsibility for your wrongdoings.
(High school senior)

Be patient. Things will come to you,
though you can guide them on your way.
(High school senior)

Quit social media. It is not worth it.
Read a book, *any book* in its stead.
(High school senior)

School might not make everyone smarter,
but the gym makes everyone stronger.
(High school senior)

Embrace change. It's the only constant.
(High school senior)

You need to discover your reasons for working hard
and develop intrinsic motivation.
(High school senior)

Get off the internet and find a passion for reading, history, art, writing, or anything like that.
Also, take all your notes with pen and paper.
(High school senior)

Act more confident.
(High school senior)

Start planning out your high school activities before 8ᵗʰ grade. You need a plan and a "passion project."
(High school senior)

Do not stress too much about small setbacks and mistakes.
(High school senior)

Take time to find a good group of people to ground you. It's also okay to change your friends along the way because you matter the most.
(High school senior)

Have a goal and work towards it.
(High school senior)

Don't let up on an opportunity to learn.
(High school senior)

Enjoy your time as a student.
(High school senior)

Work, play hard. Keep a balance.
(High school senior)

Go with the flow, and don't limit yourself to any boundaries.
(High school senior)

Learn how to manage time.
(High school senior)

YOLO (You Only Live Once).
Do what you want to do. You will be a lot happier.
(High school senior)

Walk your path.
(High school senior)

You might think being stupid is cool, but it's not. The
stuff you're doing now will affect you forever, so be
careful.
(High school senior)

Don't procrastinate.
(High school sophomore)

Be kind, but don't be so kind as to let others step on
you. Figuratively, of course.
(High school sophomore)

Be a child for as long as possible.
(High school sophomore)

Don't be so quick to trust.
Be more trusting of yourself and your feelings.
(High school sophomore)

Don't underestimate yourself.
The second you do is the second that
you are vulnerable to being hurt
and never recovering.
(High school sophomore)

Don't ever stop trying.
(High school sophomore)

Motivation promotes performance.
So find something or someone that keeps
you in shape with reality.
(High school sophomore)

Talk and discuss civilly and politely and
disagree civilly as well.
(High school sophomore)

Don't be afraid to make mistakes because
mistakes often teach us the life lessons
we need to succeed.
(High school sophomore)

Appreciate everything you have, and
don't take anything for granted.
(High school sophomore)

Your main support should be yourself, always. Trust yourself, work hard to make yourself healthier and happier, not anybody else, because others are not living your life. You are.
(High school sophomore)

What conclusions can you draw
about this group's advice?

Vicenarians

❧

Do not rush growing up. I spent so much of my teen
years wanting to be "grown" because I swore adulting
would be fun, but the reality hit harder than expected.
Between the bills, responsibility, working, and building relationships, it's much harder than the movies
depicted. I wish I had just taken the time
to enjoy being a kid.
(Rodneiyka Thornton)

Don't take life too seriously.
Your past does not define your future.
(Chris Hopper)

Do not be influenced by what you see on social media.
(Evan Kraus)

Try to practice good communication skills
and be kind to everyone.
(Kamilla Wieckowski)

❧

What conclusions can you draw
about this group's advice?

Tricenarians

❧

Don't allow pop culture to define "success" for you.
Seek to discover your life's mission, and everyday work
to advance your life through purpose and passion.
(Mordecai Ian Brownlee)

Learn to work with people.
You would be surprised what you can accomplish.
(Neftali Perez)

❧

*What conclusions can you draw
about this group's advice?*

Quadragenarians

There is an incredible amount of data and information available to you. Be informed intentionally, don't let it paralyze or consume you. Choose outlets carefully, including one that is not always aligned with your worldview.
(Anjali Jain Lueck)

Leave the world a better place
in as many places as you can.
(Todd Hoover)

Never give up on yourself and the goals you want to accomplish, no matter how many roadblocks you may encounter. If there is a will, there is a way, and you can do it.
(Veronica Thomas-Gladden)

Examine your motivations and find your own why. Then
choose selectively whom you take advice from.
(Hillary Perry Coley)

Question everything, and don't be afraid to change if
you find a truth you didn't previously know. Understand
there is truth, and it's our job to find and defend it.
(Leonard Lay)

Make kindness, empathy, and listening
actions you practice every day.
(Clare Aronow)

⁂

*What conclusions can you draw
about this group's advice?*

Quinquagenarians

You have the power to be anyone, go any place, and do anything you want. You just have to work hard and know who you are, where you want to go, and what you want to do.
(Ann Pearson)

Realize that, regardless of what you have been told, you are not the center of the universe.
(Matthew Mitchell)

The first piece of advice is never to give unsolicited advice. Before you pass final judgment on anyone or anything, wait. Waiting and hoping are beautiful, wonderful things and will sustain you even if you hate yourself, don't believe in yourself, and feel like the whole world is against you.
(Mark Johnson)

You do make a difference. I know you think it's
not worth trying to change things. But you are the
change. You are so close to beginning your watch. Know
how important you are to this world and what will come
of it/us.
(Robin Fitzpatrick)

Do not defend your oppressors,
no matter their race or gender.
(Linnie S. Carter)

Don't get frustrated or angry, and quit until you have
secured a new opportunity. Look for opportunities, and
then wisely plan your transitions.
(Mike Hall)

We live the quality of life we think we deserve. If one
believes their value is minimal, they live life this way
and will settle and exist for less. If one recognizes their
unique skills, talents, and specialness and has self-
awareness of these values, their lives will thrive through
higher expectations.
(Mike Molla)

Follow your passion. Explore, meet as many people as
possible, try as many things as possible, learn from others, and do what you love. Money often follows versus
the other way around!
(Scott Esser)

Relationships matter in everything you do in life
(personal and professional). Relationships create
meaning in your life.
They require work, but it's worth it.
(Steve Nunez)

Save early for your future. Give, serve,
and contribute to projects that are different.
(L. Marshall Washington)

Wherever you are, whatever you are doing, whomever
you are with, maximize the moment. You can't change
the past; the future will be determined by how you
engage the present.
(Jennifer Billman)

Future generations need to learn from the successes
and failures of the past, or they will likely repeat ill-
advised approaches. Reflect on your successes and
failures and find your strengths and resiliency
in those lessons.
(David Tracy)

Take the time to learn who you are, your beliefs, and
your passions. Learn to be comfortable and confident
in your body, not someone else's.
(B. Starr Simpson)

Put your phone down and enjoy the presence of
the person in front of you.
(Lisa Duke)

❧

*What conclusions can you draw
about this group's advice?*

Sexagenarians

❦

If you think you have all the answers,
you're not asking enough questions.
(Maria Mark)

Invest time in your family members,
both nuclear and extended.
You'll likely need them someday.
(Paul Herman)

Hold on tightly to your integrity against the onslaught
of outside judgments and criticisms-especially if you are
an empathetic soul.
(Janet Kemmerer)

If you wake up in the morning and don't feel happy
when your feet hit the floor, there's something wrong
in your life.
Fix it.
(Chris Lester)

Don't let other people's roadblocks stop you from
reaching your goals.
(Bruce Cleary)

Help other people, and you will be fulfilled.
(Curtis Ford)

Believe in yourself.
(John J. "Ski" Sygielski)

Compromise is sometimes necessary
for relationship building.
This applies to people, companies, and governments.
(Timothy Sandoe)

Always say yes when asked to do something or given an
opportunity. You never know who or what circumstances
may be involved, but they will always come back and
open doors for you. You never know who's watching.
(Thomas Long)

Take care of yourself. Keep your family close. Enjoy life.
When you make a mistake, embrace, and celebrate what
you learned.
(Anonymous)

Learn, understand, and use our government, your
relationships, the environments in which you work and

live, and your talents to make the region where you live a better place. Understand the strengths, weaknesses, opportunities, and threats of where you live to make it a better place for future generations.
(Dave Black)

Don't let others dictate your life.
(Janet Quigley-Abbott)

Be bold. Life is short. Dream big and don't be afraid to act on those dreams.
(Lori Sundberg)

Learn to write well, be curious, and respect everyone around you.
(Joseph Robinson, Jr.)

Life is a journey. Take it one step at a time. Along the way, be your best, be real, kind, and smart. Know that your decisions and actions may matter later.
(Ellen Glasser)

What conclusions can you draw about this group's advice?

Septuagenarians

Take care of this earth.
(We should have done it for you.)
(Eileen Krimsky)

As you transition into adult roles, don't get so serious or
cynical that you lose the sense of playfulness you had as
a child or the idealism you had as an adolescent.
(Joe Cuseo)

Sharing your faith with family, friends, and others is
how to live a life that gives and receives joy.
(Lana G. Rinaman)

Realize that every decision a person makes is based on
what they have experienced in life and their knowledge
of the topic.
If you disagree, don't argue, but listen and
engage in dialogue.
(Lynne Norton)

Never stop learning and being curious.
(Kathy Hodges)

Live outside yourself, and focus on benefiting others
even, if needed, at your own expense.
(Don R. Lynn)

Get all the education you can. You must never consider
yourself learned but instead, a lifelong learner.
(Preston Hodges)

Let mentors provide guidance. They believe in you, and
you must believe in yourself. Say often to yourself, "I
can, and I will." A positive attitude gets you anywhere.
(Toni Cleveland)

When a decision is to be made, make it with solid
advice, data, and insight. Being a decisive leader cannot
be underestimated. Also, your "gut" often knows what
is right and true. And remember, it is not the decision
itself but how it is communicated.
It is not the what; it's the how.
(Irene Kovala)

*What conclusions can you draw
about this group's advice?*

Octogenarians

I offer my grandmother's advice: Make yourself useful.
(Sharon Scholl)

Be part of the solution, not the problem. We were given
two eyes, two ears, and one mouth.
(Sally Clemens)

Ground your soul in life.
(Kim Rinaman)

You will be confronted with problems and roadblocks
along life's way. Do not give up. Persevere.
(David R. Johnson)

Constantly, vigorously, and with intentional
forethought, practice loving-kindness with no caveats or
limitations.
Love your neighbor and value all humans.
(Alexander "Sandy" Berry)

Determine in your mind the major issues of the day
and how they affect society or humanity as a whole.
Concerns like climate change, income and wealth
inequalities, educational inequalities, roles individuals
can play in solving these problems, the role government
policies can play in solving these problems, and reli-
gious intolerance.
In disagreements, try to understand the opposing view.
(Bob Fuller)

*What conclusions can you draw
about this group's advice?*

Nonagenarians

If you have a goal or passion you want, don't be stopped
by the advice of others. Two of the most important
decisions in my life I was advised against...Fortunately, I
did not heed that advice.
I would also tell those younger that I regret that our
generation and those before us have been careless with
our environment and resources. We have left those
who follow us with tough problems—global warming,
population growth, migration, and dysfunctional
governing structures. I think you of the next generation
will need resilience, sacrifice, and vision.
(Joan S. Carver)

Life isn't about me. It's about others.
(Frances Bartlett Kinne)

When it comes to raising children, give a little bit of love
and a little bit of discipline. Balance is important.
(Frances Mascola)

Have some kind of faith and respect for everyone and
show acceptance. You may not like someone,
but you don't have to be nasty.
(Fran Bartlett)

*What conclusions can you draw
about this group's advice?*

Centenarians

❦

Exercise. Keep moving!
(Jo Gilbert)

❦

*What conclusions can you draw
about this centenarian advice?*

Takeaways and Perspectives

❧

BEFORE YOU MOVE ON TO the next section, pause and reflect on the responses you just read. Engage a friend, colleague, family member, or community representative in a dialogue for their perspectives. Use the following as conversation starters:

* What similarities did you detect from group to group?
* What striking differences stood out between the age groups?
* What takeaway(s) do you have after reading the wisdom responses?

The Questions

As you look ahead to your future, what ONE QUESTION would you like to ask those older than you? (What is something you are curious about?)

Kiddiegenarians

❧

What teacher will I have for 3rd grade?
(2nd Grader)

What will my day be like as a 3rd grader?
(2nd Grader)

Will my 3rd-grade teacher always be nice?
(2nd Grader)

What is the hardest thing in 3rd grade?
Times tables or division or nothing?
(2nd Grader)

Will 3rd grade be "funner" than 2nd grade?
(2nd Grader)

I want to be an author like you. How?
(2nd Grader)

What are we going to learn in science?
(2nd Grader)

What is 3rd grade like?
(2nd Grader)

Is the teacher going to give out candy?
(2nd Grader)

*What conclusions can you draw
about this group's questions?*

Denarians

Have you ever been to a point where you were generally
happy and stress-free?
(High school senior)

Did anything improve in the future?
Has the world become a better place at all?
(High school senior)

Are you happy with the person you've become?
Or is that irrelevant to what you want to achieve?
(High school senior)

Is there ever a point in life where you have realized you
are satisfied with your current state of life?
(High school senior)

Do things get better?
(High school senior)

How do you stay positive in your outlook,
even when things look dim?
(High school senior)

What were you thinking about designing American cit-
ies and towns around cars rather than people?
(High school senior)

How do you do taxes?
(High school senior)

How do you pass the time and keep mentally sharp
in the worst circumstances?
(High school senior)

How do you deal with the freedom and responsibilities
of full-on adulthood? Isn't it overwhelming?
(High school senior)

How do I get the most back on my tax return
and maximize retirement?
(High school senior)

Do old regrets still weigh you down,
or do they fade away?
(High school senior)

What is your biggest regret about your youth?
(High school senior)

How do you find the motivation to complete your goals?
(High school senior)

Is where you are now your definition of successful?
(High school senior)

What is your biggest regret in life? (Don't tell me you
don't have any because I know you do.)
(High school senior)

How different has your life been compared to what
you envisioned when you were a teen?
(High school senior)

How do you keep your motivation?
(High school senior)

I want to know how to find out what I want to do
for the rest of my life.
(High school senior)

How do you find motivation?
(High school senior)

Does getting older make people change their mindsets,
or does that depend on each person? So many adults
tell me that my "young spirit" will go away with age,
but I don't know if that's true.
(High school senior)

How did you manage time better?
(High school senior)

How do I know what I want to do for the rest of my life?
(High school senior)

How to be successful after college?
What are the steps you took to avoid going bankrupt?
(High school senior)

How were you able to grab motivation at your lowest?
(High school sophomore)

How long did it take for you to find a point
to settle down in life?
(High school sophomore)

How was it fun in high school?
(High school sophomore)

Why do you push your issues as a community,
on to younger generations?
(High school sophomore)

Does the constant hustle ever stop?
(High school sophomore)

Anything you would do differently?
(High school sophomore)

Will I ever truly stop doubting myself and my
capabilities?
(High school sophomore)

How do you figure out problems so calmly and
efficiently?
(High school sophomore)

Is the present more important to you than the future?
(High school sophomore)

Is it better to chase success or happiness?
(High school sophomore)

Honestly, what is worth spending time on
to be more specific in college?
(High school sophomore)

Are you afraid of growing up?
Do you ever feel like life is going too fast?
(High school sophomore)

❧

*What conclusions can you draw
about this group's questions?*

Vicenarians

How do you maintain so much peace in the middle of the storms? That's a question I constantly asked my grandmother, who would be going through some hard times, and through it all, she kept her peace and faith strong.
(Rodneiyka Thornton)

What has given you the most happiness in life?
(Chris Hopper)

How do you not get caught up in the daily monotony of work and responsibilities?
How do you keep life interesting?
(Evan Kraus)

Throughout your life, what social movement
impacted you the most?
(Kamilla Wieckowski)

❧

*What conclusions can you draw
about this group's questions?*

Tricenarians

❦

What were the avoidable mistakes that
somehow you failed to avoid?
(Mordecai Ian Brownlee)

I never understood how retirement works. You retire
with a fixed income, but what happens if that income
depletes, and you are still alive, have no one to take care
of you, and have no money to pay for a nursing home?
(Neftali Perez)

❦

*What conclusions can you draw
about this group's questions?*

Quadragenarians

How do you find a balance between active engagement
to effect change and cultivating a quiet peace
and acceptance in the now?
(Anjali Jain Lueck)

If you had your life to live over again, what is the one
thing you would redo, and what is the one thing
you would not redo, and why?
(Todd Hoover)

At what stage in life, if ever, do you get over the fear and
stress about what others think of you? Is it age 50? Or
after grandchildren. Or after you have accomplished all
that you wanted and the opinions of others
no longer bind you to established acceptances?
(Veronica Thomas-Gladden)

How did you define meaning in your life as you left the workforce, your children grew up and created their own lives, and your friends passed away? Where did your life satisfaction come from when aging?
(Hillary Perry Coley)

Do you believe you could have done anything in the past that would've made you live a happier life?
(Leonard Lay)

What has been your favorite decade of life and why?
(Clare Aronow)

❧

What conclusions can you draw
about this group's questions?

Quinquagenarians

What was the most exciting destination you ever visited
and why did you go?
(Ann Pearson)

How are we (Generation X) doing? Were you as fright-
ened for the future of the country as we are?
(Matthew Mitchell)

If, on your deathbed, you were given a chance to go
back to the age of 18 and live a second life without
knowing how or when it would end up, would you take
that second chance?
(Mark Johnson)

If I needed to stop everything right now to attend to the
most important thing in life, what was that to you?
(Robin Fitzpatrick)

Who or what would you risk it all for and why?
(Linnie S. Carter)

Do you recommend retiring or just moving into some
other activity that you are passionate about?
(Mike Hall)

What should I know, and then live life accordingly,
that I am unaware of asking?
(Mike Molla)

Any regrets in life or things you wish
you would have done?
(Scott Esser)

If you could alter one decision you made,
what would it be and why?
(Steve Nunez)

What can we do to solve the distance
that is between so many?
(L. Marshall Washington)

How does what you look for in life now differ from
when you were younger and why?
(Jennifer Billman)

What has sustained you during your most uncertain and dire circumstances? What strategies proved most effective in your successes and failures?
(David Tracy)

How did you do it? (Whatever your 'it' is.)
(B. Starr Simpson)

What is golden about the golden years?
(Lisa Duke)

What one thing would you have done differently in the years leading up to retirement?
(Dan Whitford)

❧

What conclusions can you draw
about this group's questions?

Sexagenarians

When do you walk away from something you love to do
that has been a big part of your identity?
(Thomas Long)

Are you where you imagined yourself to be right now?
(Maria Mark)

Do your views on a potential afterlife deepen or change
as you approach the end of your earthly existence?
(Paul Herman)

Do you fear death?
(Bruce Cleary)

How do you develop the wisdom to determine when to
hold on to and when to let go of difficult issues?
(Janet Kemmerer)

Do you think our world is better or worse for the adoption of smartphones by most of the world's population?
(Curtis Ford)

If you were to relive your life,
what one thing would you do differently?
(John J. "Ski" Sygielski)

What methods did you use to adapt to change?
(Timothy Sandoe)

What was your best decade and why?
(Anonymous)

What is the best way to stay connected, stay involved, and do good things (at my own pace) in a serious, productive way?
(Dave Black)

Did you achieve most of what you wanted in life?
(Janet Quigley-Abbott)

Why does there always have to be a *we/them* division
to all things of any importance?
Why is there always an *in-group* and an *out-group*?
(Lori Sundberg)

Do you have many regrets about the way your life
turned out?
Are you contented?
(Joseph Robinson, Jr)

Who are your heroes, and why?
(Ellen Glasser)

❧

*What conclusions can you draw
about this group's questions?*

Septuagenarians

To my grandfather, who left Russia alone as a 16-year-old Jew running from the Czar: How did you find the courage to leave everyone and everything you knew, and why didn't you tell us about your experiences? All your grandchildren want to know, and none of your children had answers for us.
(Eileen Krimsky)

Since I'm already old (72), I'd ask those in their 80s and 90s if and how their views of life, death, and an afterlife have changed as they move closer to the end of life.
(Joe Cuseo)

Do you think your faith has grown because of your experience or your study?
(Lana G. Rinaman)

What are your answers to
questions 1 (Lesson) and 2 (Advice) above?
(Lynne Norton)

What are your greatest joys? Regrets?
(Kathy Hodges)

When do the person reflected in the mirror and the
person looking into that same mirror find contentment
and/or understanding?
(Don R. Lynn)

How do they contemplate not having a human experience, and how do they envision a spiritual experience?
(Preston Hodges)

Do they believe the country will become
a gentler, kinder nation?
(Toni Cleveland)

How do you find balance and perspective? When life
(read: work) seems all-consuming, how do you find
moments to pause for clarity and with purpose?
(Irene Kovala)

❦

*What conclusions can you draw
about this group's questions?*

Octogenarians

How will you satisfyingly conclude your life?
(Sharon Scholl)

What traits should be developed to be successful?
(Sally Clemens)

Is your peace in service or faith?
(Kim Rinaman)

What actions have you taken to enrich the lives of
those you know and love, as well as others perhaps less
fortunate?
(David R. Johnson)

How do they deal with the approaching end-of-life
condition? What are their practices as they approach
each day?
How do they communicate with family and friends?
How do they show loving-kindness?
(Alexander "Sandy" Berry)

At 85 years old, I have no older friends or relatives to
ask for their wisdom. Nor am I intellectually rigor-
ous enough to come up with many questions an older
generation might have answers to. When questions
come to mind, and I am seriously curious about an
answer, I know that many very smart people likely have
researched and written about the subject. I know I can
find an answer if I am honest, diligent, and patient.
(Bob Fuller)

❧

*What conclusions can you draw
about this group's questions?*

Nonagenarians

❧

How do you maintain optimism about the future and
the years ahead when you face the loss of friends,
relatives, good health, and usefulness?
(Joan S. Carver)

What is your call to action to help others?
How will you make it about others, not yourself?
(Frances Bartlett Kinne)

If we remove some of the technology, will that allow
respect and human connections to grow again?
(Frances Mascola)

Why are people so unhappy with their own life
that it leads to disrespect and nastiness?
(Fran Bartlett)

∞

*What conclusions can you draw
about this group's questions?*

Centenarians

❧

I don't know anyone older than me.
But I would ask them what they did to get this old!
(Jo Gilbert)

❧

What conclusions can you draw
from this centenarian question?

Takeaways and Perspectives

❦

BEFORE YOU MOVE ON TO the next section, pause and reflect on the responses you just read. Engage a friend, colleague, family member, or community representative in a dialogue for their perspectives. Use the following as conversation starters:

- What similarities did you detect from group to group?
- What striking differences stood out between the age groups?
- What takeaway(s) do you have after reading the wisdom responses?

Takeaways: One Perspective

❦

On PAGE 18, I CHALLENGED you to consider the takeaways from the three questions for each age group. While wisdom differs from person to person, does it vary from generation to generation? If you discover such variations, perhaps that diversity and contrast of offerings can lead to deliberative dialogues for understanding, appreciation, and learning.

Beginning on the next page, you will find my perspective. Like a conversation you might have with a book club about *Sharing Wisdom Across the Ages*, my offerings may contradict or complement your interpretations. Similarly, as you read the preceding pages, you may have stopped and embraced a particular piece of sage advice or an intriguing lesson. Or, you may have found yourself shaking your head at someone's so-called wisdom. Whether you drew closer to or stepped further away from the words, each response provided an opportunity to see perspectives that support or challenge our experiences and opinions.

I suggest you do *not* read the following pages until you have compiled your takeaways.

KIDDIEGENARIANS (9-YEAR-OLDS & UNDER)

* Lesson:
  o Recent classroom instruction leaves an impression.
* Advice:
  o Listen to your teachers and learn the rules.
* Question:
  o What will the immediate future look like?

DENARIANS (10- TO 19-YEAR-OLDS)

* Lesson:
  o Respect yourself and your social connections.
* Advice:
  o Build self-awareness, self-respect, and self-discipline.
* Question:
  o How do you discover and maximize success and happiness?

VICENARIANS (20- TO 29-YEAR-OLDS)

- Lesson:
  - o Be in the present and be yourself.
- Advice:
  - o Embrace the present.
- Question:
  - o How do you maintain a sense of peace, interest, and significance?

TRICENARIANS (30- TO 39-YEAR-OLDS)

- Lesson:
  - o Notice what people do.
- Advice:
  - o Discover yourself and those around you.
- Question:
  - o How do you prepare for the future and avoid the unavoidable?

QUADRAGENARIANS (40- TO 49-YEAR-OLDS)

- Lesson:
  - o Since life will change, pay attention and pivot as necessary.

* Advice:
  o Be mindful, adjust, and grow.
* Question:
  o How do you find balance, peace, and happiness?

QUINQUAGENARIANS (50- TO 59-YEAR-OLDS)

* Lesson:
  o Question career/life motives and decisions.
* Advice:
  o Be present and grow from and with your connections and experiences.
* Question:
  o What would you do differently?

SEXAGENARIANS (60- TO 69-YEAR-OLDS)

* Lesson:
  o Life is cumulative. Pay attention.
* Advice:
  o Explore and stay curious.
* Question:
  o What have you learned from the past and what should we expect of the future?

Septuagenarians (70- to 79-year-olds)

- Lesson:
  - o Small things are big things.
- Advice:
  - o Respect others and be accountable.
- Question:
  - o How did you and how should we find and cultivate personal peace?

Octogenarians (80- to 89-year-olds)

- Lesson:
  - o Life unfolds.
- Advice:
  - o Be useful, kind, and humble.
- Question:
  - o What have you done to help others while you prepare for the end of life?

Nonagenarians (90- to 99-year-olds)

- Lesson:
  - o While the family is important, cherish and nurture personal independence.

- Advice:
  - o Respect yourself and others.
- Question:
  - o Can we cultivate optimism over nastiness?

Centenarians (100- to 109-year-olds)

- Lesson: Stay active.
- Advice: Stay active.
- Question: What did you do to get this old?

Final Words

After reading all this, you might ask, "Steve, what is your wisdom? How do you answer the three questions?"

With humility and deference to all of the preceding wise thoughts, I offer:

LESSON:

I have been and continue to be a work in progress. There have been and will continue to be discoveries, do-overs, and daily opportunities to understand who I am. Happiness comes from within, not from without.

ADVICE:

If you want your dreams to become a reality, you must embark on a journey of reflection and action. And you must set, recognize, and respect your boundaries and limits on that journey.

QUESTION:

How have you remained relevant as you have aged?

Appendix A:
The Demographics

Who participated in this "study"? What did the respondents look like from a demographic standpoint?[19] The following descriptors come directly from the respondents. Neither the author nor reviewers of this book have altered those responses. Even when two terms might be considered the same (such as "White" and "Caucasian"), whatever the respondent wrote is reflected here. Is there any wisdom in the self-identified labels? Perhaps therein lies another considered conversation with one of your pods.

---

[19] As noted earlier in this book, the participants do not represent a scientific sampling. The Kiddiegenarian group did not respond to race or ethnicity questions.

Total Participants:

* 127

Age Groupings[20]

* *Kiddiegenarians*[21] (9-year-olds & under)
  o 26
* *Denarians* (10- to 19-year-olds)
  o 39
* *Vicenarians* (20- to 29-year-olds)
  o 04
* *Tricenarians* (30- to 39-year-olds)
  o 02
* *Quadragenarians* (40- to 49-year-olds)
  o 06
* *Quinquagenarians* (50- to 59-year-olds)
  o 15
* *Sexagenarians* (60- to 69-year-olds)
  o 15
* *Septuagenarians* (70- to 79-year-olds)
  o 09

---

20 In a few instances, people who responded were in one age group when they submitted their thoughts to the author and by the time the book was published they moved into the next grouping. For example, one respondent was 69 years old at the time of response; he is now 70 years old. In instances like this, the recorded age represents the age at answer submission.

21 See footnote #4.

- *Octogenarians* (80- to 89-year-olds)
  - o 06
- *Nonagenarians* (90- to 99-year-olds)
  - o 04
- *Centenarians* (100- to 109-year-olds)
  - o 01

Gender
The respondents self-identified as:

- Female
  - o 63
- Male
  - o 61
- Non-binary
  - o 03

Race[22]
The respondents self-identified as:

- African American
  - o 02
- American
  - o 01

---

[22] The numbers do not add up to 127 (total number of respondents). (1) Some respondents did not answer the item or said "IDK"—I Don't Know. (2) The elementary students were not asked to self-identify.

- Arabic/White
  - o 01
- Asian
  - o 20
- Asian-American
  - o 01
- Black
  - o 05
- Black/African American
  - o 02
- Black/American
  - o 01
- Black/White
  - o 01
- Caucasian
  - o 08
- Haitian
  - o 01
- Human
  - o 01
- Indian
  - o 02
- Mestizo
  - o 01
- Mixed
  - o 01
- White
  - o 43

Ethnicity[23]

The respondents self-identified as:

- Afghanistan
  - o 01
- African American
  - o 01
- African American/European
  - o 01
- American
  - o 07
- Anglo/Irish/Scottish/German
  - o 01
- Asian
  - o 01
- Black
  - o 03
- Britain/Western European
  - o 01
- Bulgarian
  - o 01
- Caucasian
  - o 01
- Czech/Dutch
  - o 01
- Chinese
  - o 01

---

23 See footnote #22 above.

- Dominican
  - o 01
- Eastern European White
  - o 01
- English/Swedish/German/Welsh
  - o 01
- European American
  - o 02
- Filipino
  - o 07
- French
  - o 01
- German
  - o 02
- German/Anglo-Saxon
  - o 01
- Hispanic
  - o 01
- Hispanic (Colombian)
  - o 01
- Indian
  - o 09
- Irish/English Ashkenazi Jew
  - o 01
- Irish/German/English
  - o 01
- Irish/Swedish
  - o 01

- Italian
  - o 02
- Italian/Irish
  - o 01
- Italian/German
  - o 01
- Japanese
  - o 01
- Korean
  - o 02
- Latino
  - o 01
- Non-Hispanic
  - o 02
- Northern European
  - o 01
- Norwegian/German
  - o 01
- Mixed
  - o 01
- Mixed European
  - o 01
- Polish
  - o 01
- Polish/Ukrainian
  - o 01
- Russian-Jew
  - o 01

- Scotch/Irish
  - o 01
- Scots/Irish/English-7th Generation American
  - o 01
- Slovak/German
  - o 01
- South Asian
  - o 01
- Swedish/West Virginian
  - o 01
- WASP
  - o 01
- West Indian
  - o 01
- White
  - o 05
- White Caucasian
  - o 01
- White American
  - o 01
- White-Non-Hispanic
  - o 01

Occupation[24]

Of those who responded to this question, their occupations included (in alphabetical order):

---

24 A few of the early questionnaires that went out did not include the "Occupation" question. Still, you can get a feel for the respondents from this listing

- Author/speaker
- CEO
- Chaplin (retired)
- Contractor
- Dentist
- Elementary school physical education teacher (retired)
- Entrepreneur
- Executive Chef
- Geographic Information Systems Technician
- Higher Education Administrators (including presidents, vice presidents, and senior-level administrators)
- Manager
- Mayor
- Non-Profit Administrator
- Non-Profit CEO
- Parent
- Professor
- Project Analyst
- Program Coordinator
- Psychologist
- Realtor
- Retired
- Software Developer
- Student (elementary and secondary)
- Teacher
- Yoga instructor

Suggested Reading

In addition to the footnote sources found on earlier pages in this book, the following works provide wisdom to consider.

Applewhite, Ashton. *This Chair Rocks: A Manifesto Against Ageism.* New York, New York: Celadon Books, 2016.

Buettner, Dan. *The Blue Zones of Happiness: Lessons from the World's Happiest People.* Washington, D.C.: National Geographic, 2017.

Csikszentmihalyi, Mihaly. *Flow: The Psychology Of Optimal Experience.* New York, New York: Harper Perennial, 1990.

Hanson, Rick. *Buddha's Brain: The Practical Neuroscience of Happiness, Love, and Wisdom.* Oakland, CA: New Harbinger Publications, Inc., 2009.

Esty, Katherine. *Eighty Somethings: A Practical Guide to Letting Go, Aging Well, and Finding Unexpected Happiness.* New York, New York: Skyhorse Publishing, 2018.

Leland, John. *Happiness is a Choice You Make: Lessons from a Year Among the Oldest Old.* New York, New York: Sarah Crichton Books, 2018.

Marshall, Joseph M. III. *The Lakota Way: Stories and Lessons for Living. Native American Wisdom on Ethics and Character.* New York, New York: Penguin Compass, 2002.

Piscitelli, Steve, interview with Frances Bartlett Kinne, Episode #20 on The Growth and Resilience Network® podcast channel. Podcast audio, November 15, 2016. https://youtu.be/-XK6ZOuO-os.

Singer, Michael A. *Living Untethered: Beyond the Human Predicament.* Oakland, CA: New Harbinger Publications, Inc. 2022.

Singer, Michael A. *The Untethered Soul: The Journey Beyond Yourself.* Oakland, CA: New Harbinger Publications, Inc. 2007.

Tolle, Eckhart. *The Power Of Now: A Guide To Spiritual Enlightenment.* Novato, California: New World Library, 1999.

About the Author

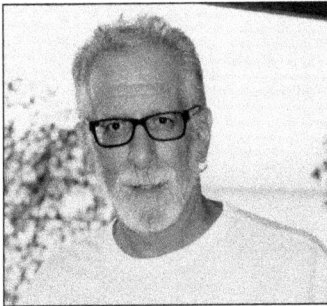

HI, I'M STEVE. THANK YOU for taking the time to read and share this book. Perhaps the questions and answers you read here will inspire you to seek and embrace the wisdom within and between your various communities.

After nearly four decades of classroom teaching and national speaking engagements, I now devote my time to writing and community-based activities. I live in Atlantic Beach, Florida, with my wife, Laurie (who remains my wisest best friend).

I love where I live, with whom I live, and what I get to do every day.

You can learn more about me, my books, videos, podcasts, and music at www.stevepiscitelli.com.

www.ingramcontent.com/pod-product-compliance
Lightning Source LLC
Chambersburg PA
CBHW061729020426
42331CB00006B/1167